THE BIG BOOK OF
EASTER MAZES

FOR KIDS

KYLE BRACH

Sky Pony Press
New York

Sky Pony Press books may be purchased in bulk at special discounts for sales promotion, corporate gifts, fund-raising, or educational purposes. Special editions can also be created to specifications. For details, contact the Special Sales Department, Sky Pony Press, 307 West 36th Street, 11th Floor, New York, NY 10018 or info@skyhorsepublishing.com.

Sky Pony® is a registered trademark of Skyhorse Publishing, Inc.®, a Delaware corporation.

Visit our website at www.skyponypress.com.

10 9 8 7 6 5 4 3 2 1

Library of Congress Cataloging-in-Publication Data is available on file.

Cover design by Bottle Cap Book Publishing Services
Cover illustrations by Shutterstock.com

Mazes licensed from mazegenerator.net

Hardcover ISBN: 978-1-5107-7476-6

Printed in China

THE BIG BOOK OF
EASTER MAZES
FOR KIDS

MAZE 1

MAZE 2

EASY

MAZE 3

MAZE 4

MAZE 5

MAZE 6

MAZE 7

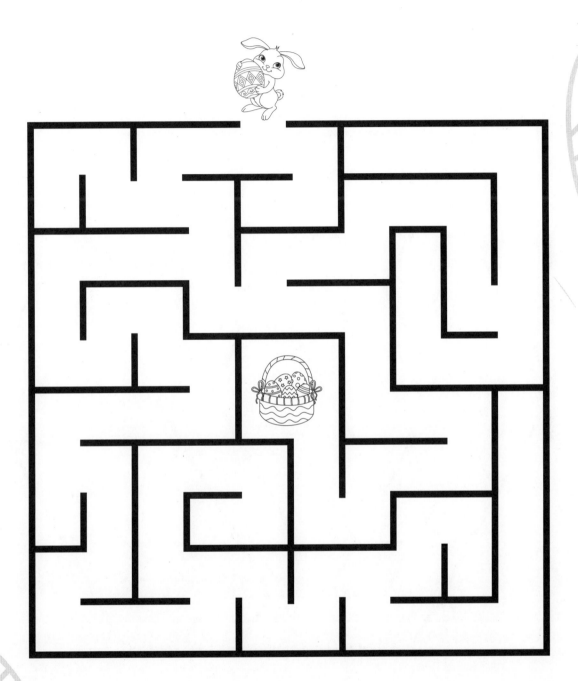

MAZE 8

EASY

MAZE 9

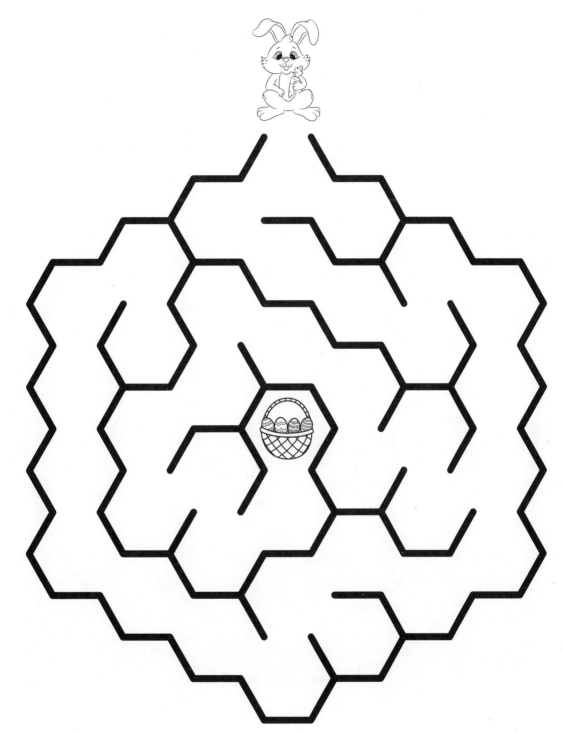

MAZE 10

EASY

MAZE 11

MAZE 12

MAZE 13

MAZE 14

MAZE 15

MAZE 16

MAZE 17

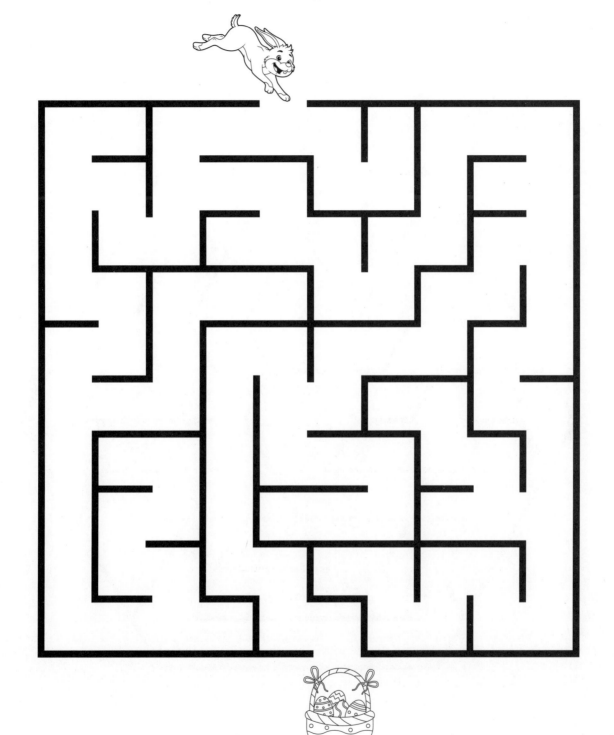

MAZE 18

MAZE 19

MAZE 20

EASY

MAZE 21

MAZE 22

MAZE 23

MAZE 24

MAZE 25

MAZE 26

MAZE 27

MAZE 28

MAZE 29

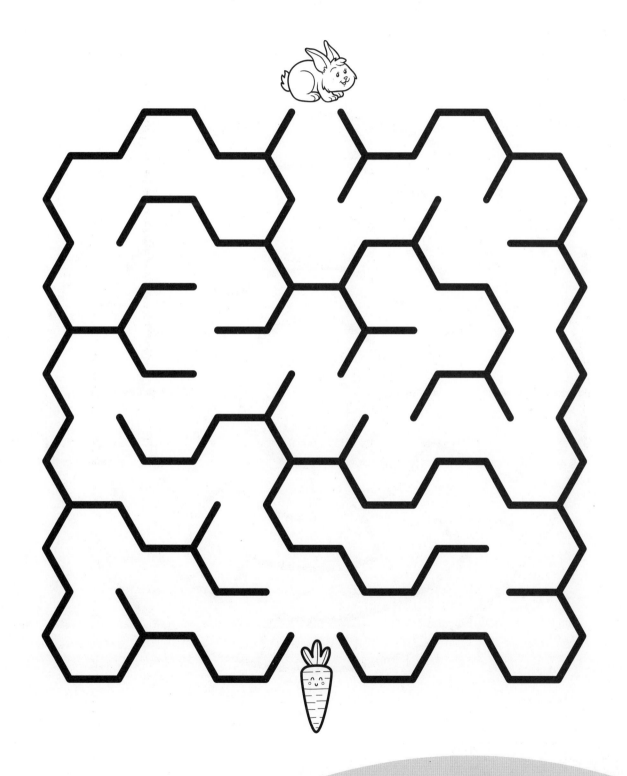

MAZE 30

MAZE 31

MAZE 32

EASY

MAZE 33

MAZE 34

EASY

MAZE 35

MAZE 36

MAZE 37

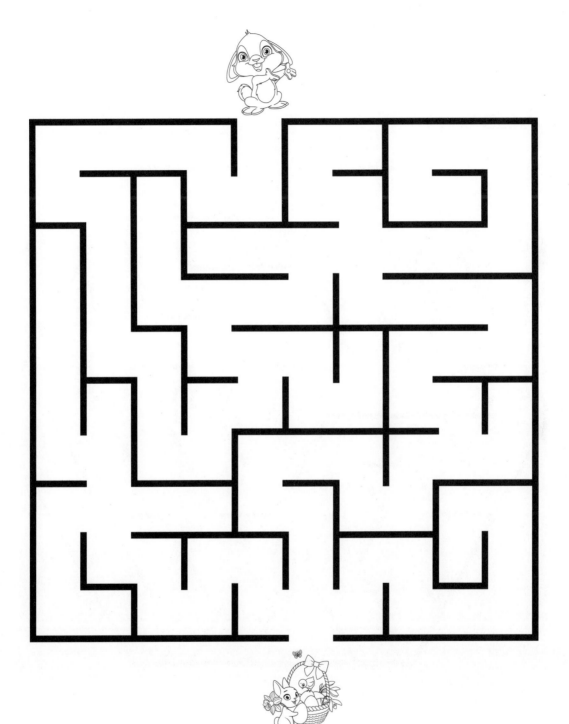

MAZE 38

MAZE 39

MAZE 40

MAZE 41

MAZE 43

MAZE 44

EASY

MAZE 45

MAZE 46

MAZE 47

MAZE 48

MAZE 49

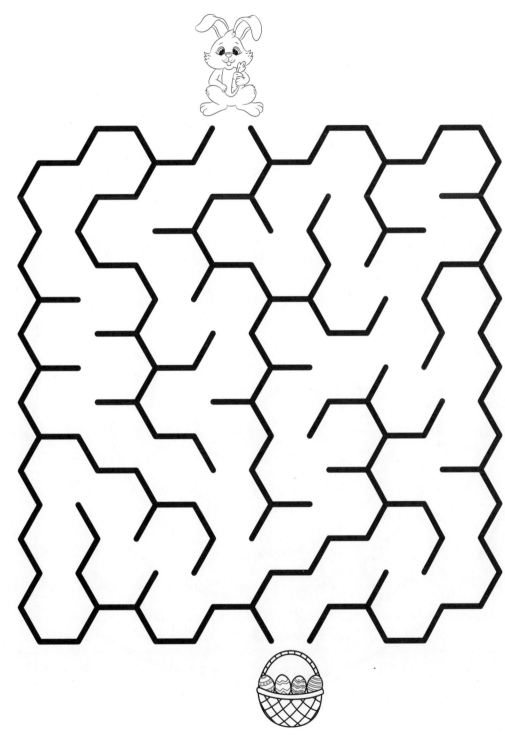

MAZE 50

MAZE 51

MAZE 52

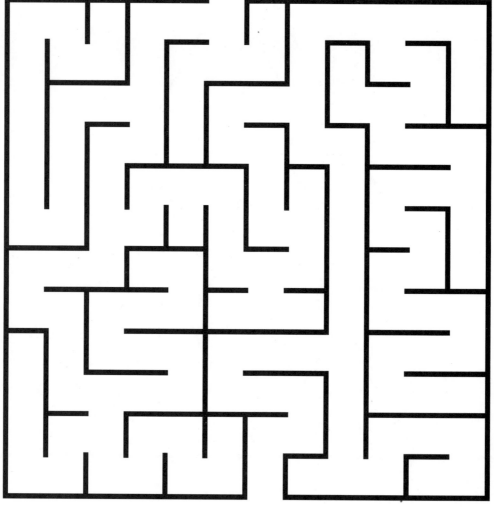

MAZE 53

MAZE 55

MAZE 56

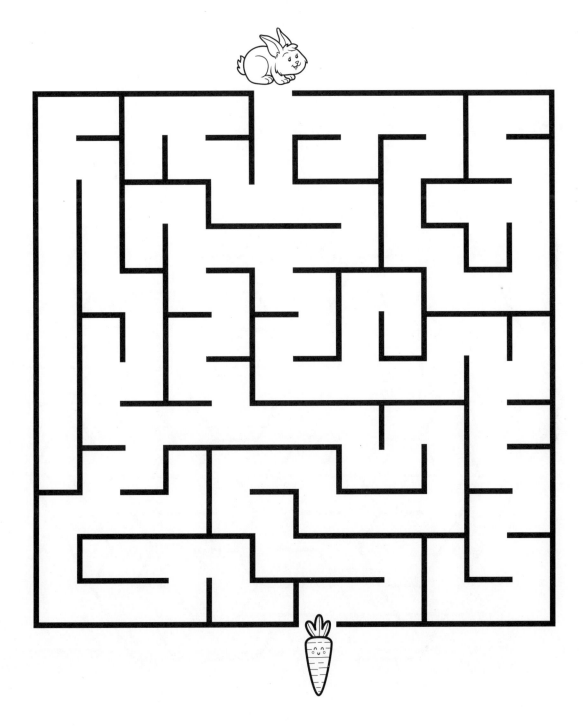

MAZE 59

MAZE 60

MAZE 61

MAZE 62

MAZE 63

MAZE 64

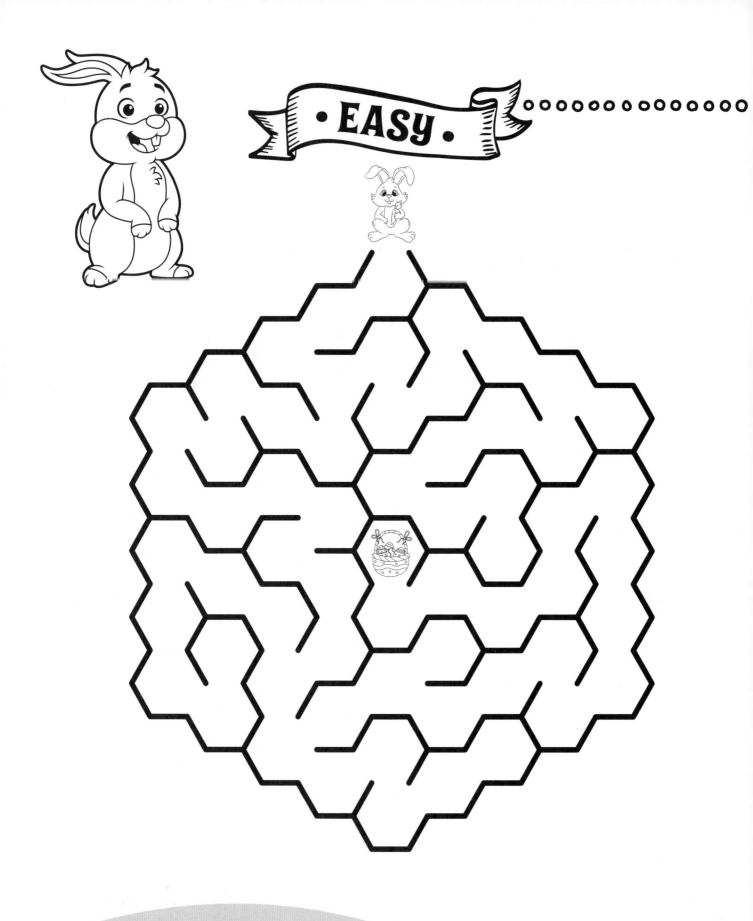

MAZE 66

MAZE 67

MAZE 68

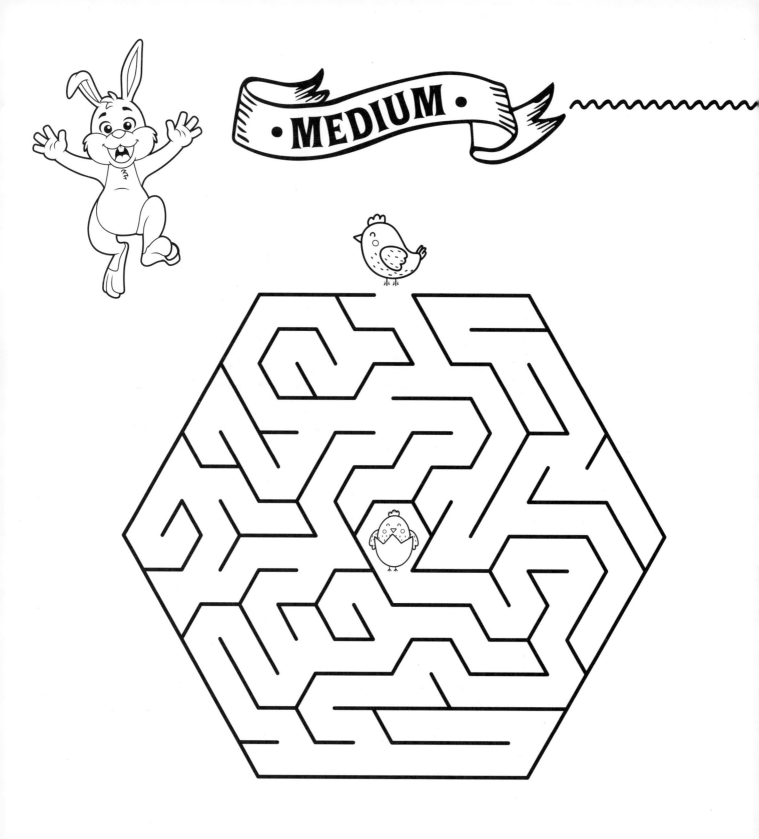

MEDIUM

MAZE 69

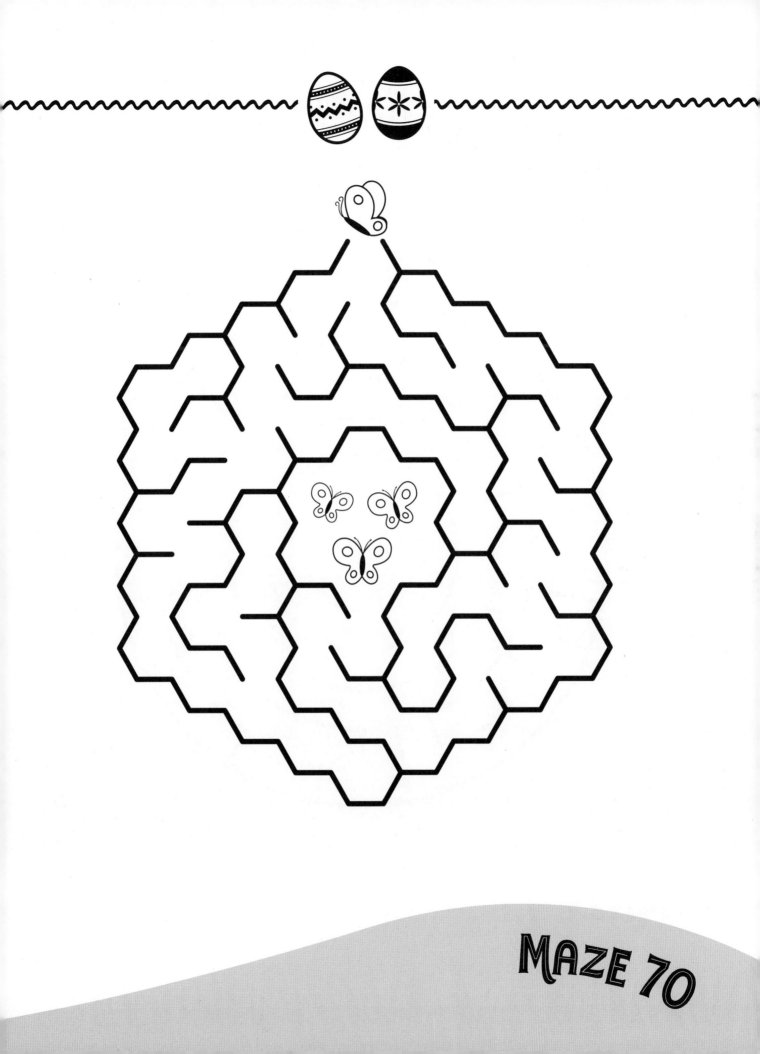

MAZE 70

MEDIUM

MAZE 71

MAZE 72

MEDIUM

MAZE 73

MAZE 74

MEDIUM

MAZE 75

MAZE 76

MEDIUM

MAZE 77

MAZE 78

MEDIUM

MAZE 79

MAZE 80

MAZE 81

MAZE 82

MEDIUM

MAZE 83

MAZE 84

MAZE 85

MEDIUM

MAZE 87

MAZE 88

MEDIUM

MAZE 89

MAZE 90

MAZE 91

MAZE 92

MEDIUM

MAZE 93

MAZE 94

MEDIUM

MAZE 95

MAZE 96

MAZE 97

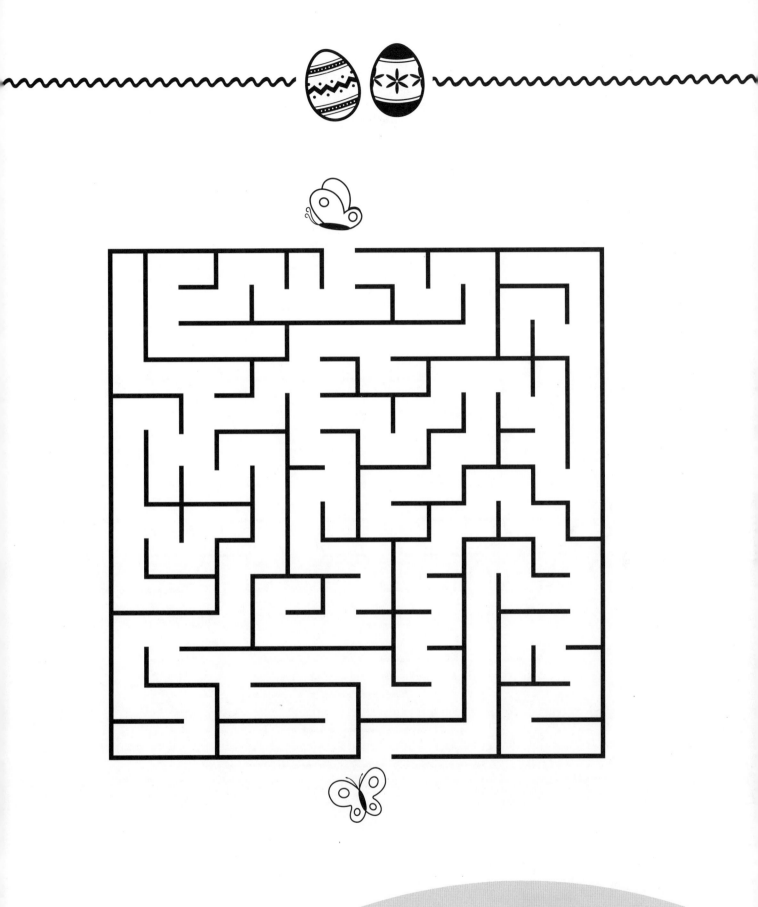

MEDIUM

MAZE 99

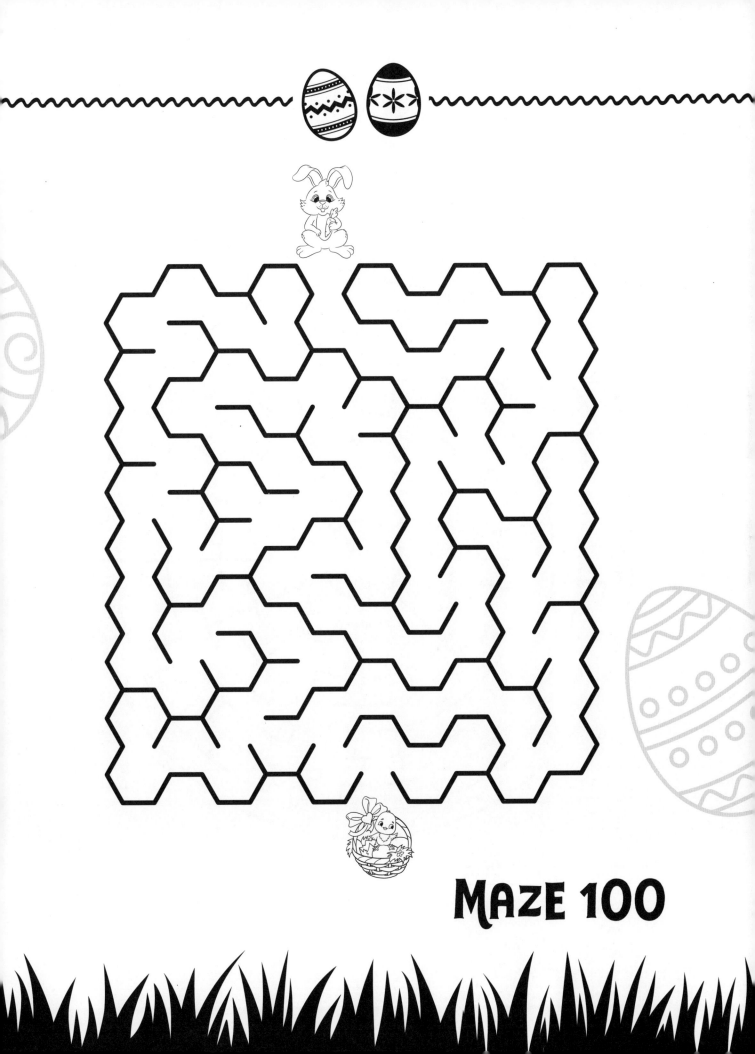

MAZE 100

MAZE 101

MAZE 102

MAZE 103

MAZE 104

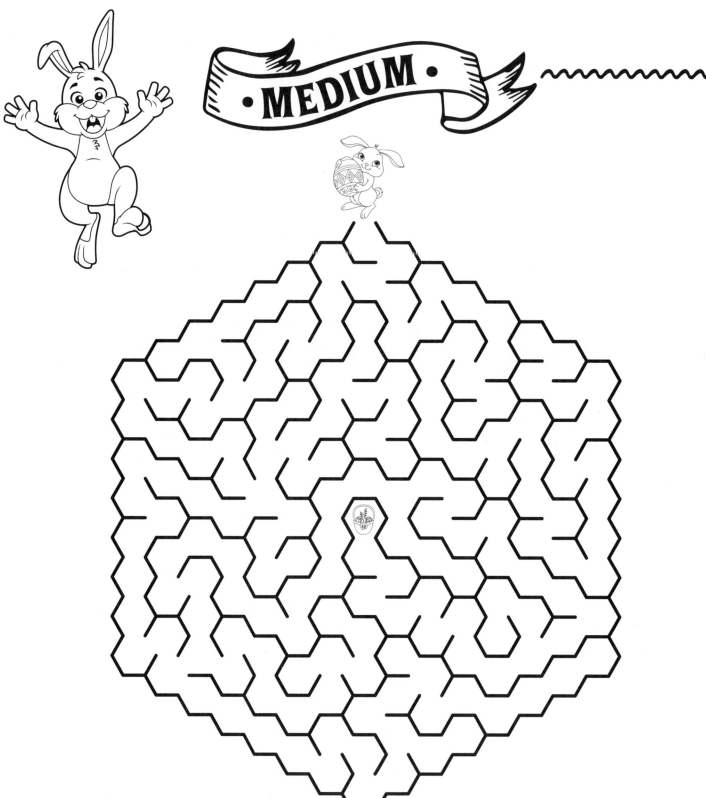

MAZE 105

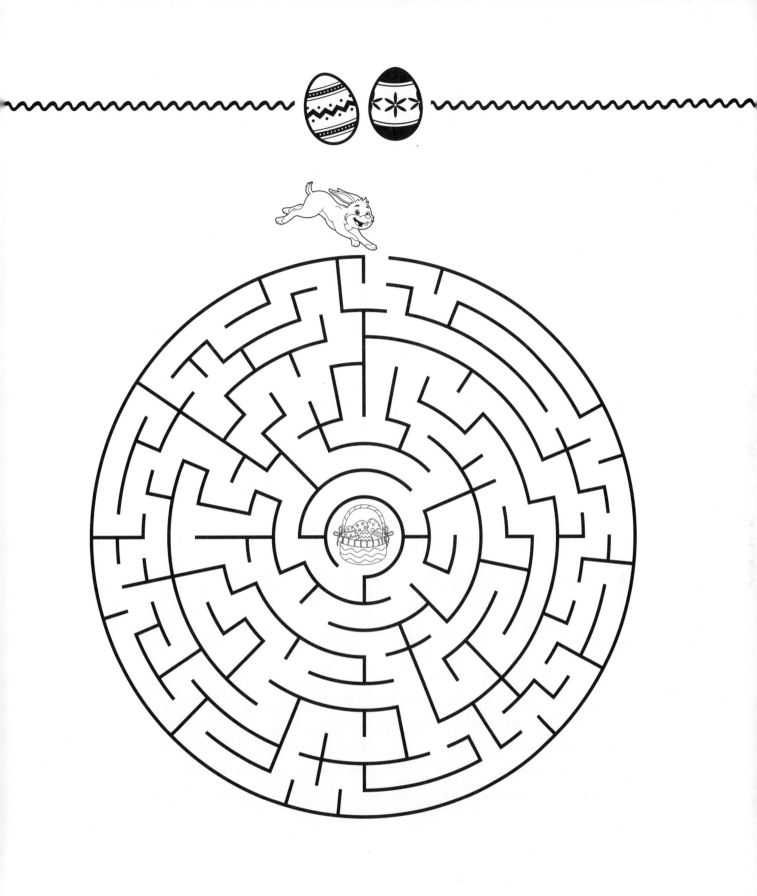

MAZE 106

MEDIUM

MAZE 107

MAZE 108

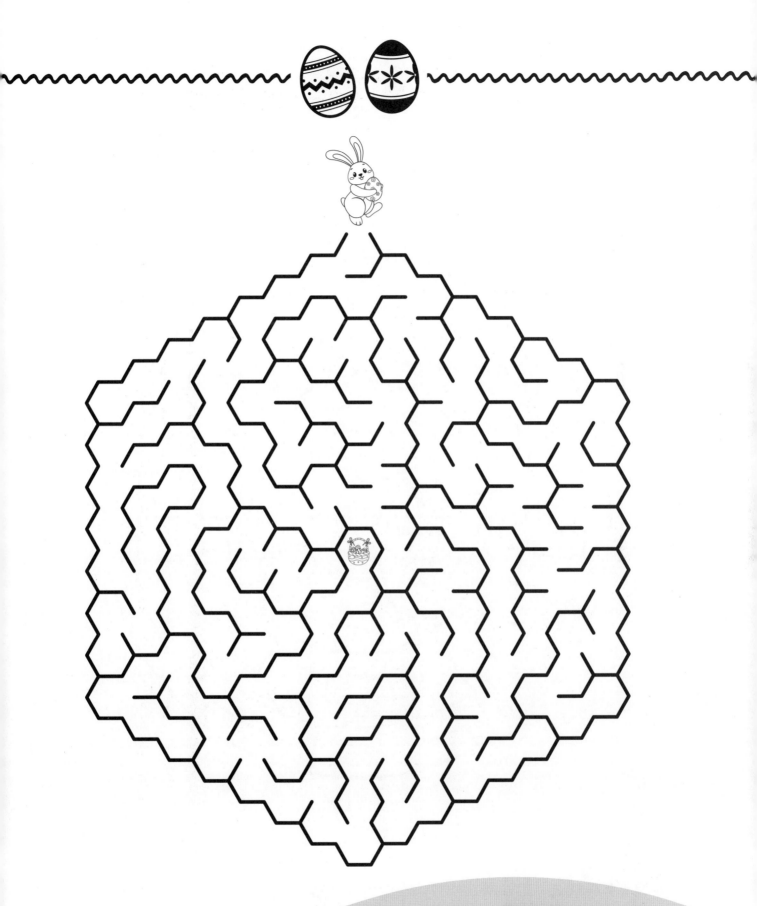

MAZE 110

MEDIUM

MAZE 111

MAZE 112

MAZE 113

MAZE 114

MEDIUM

MAZE 115

MAZE 116

MAZE 117

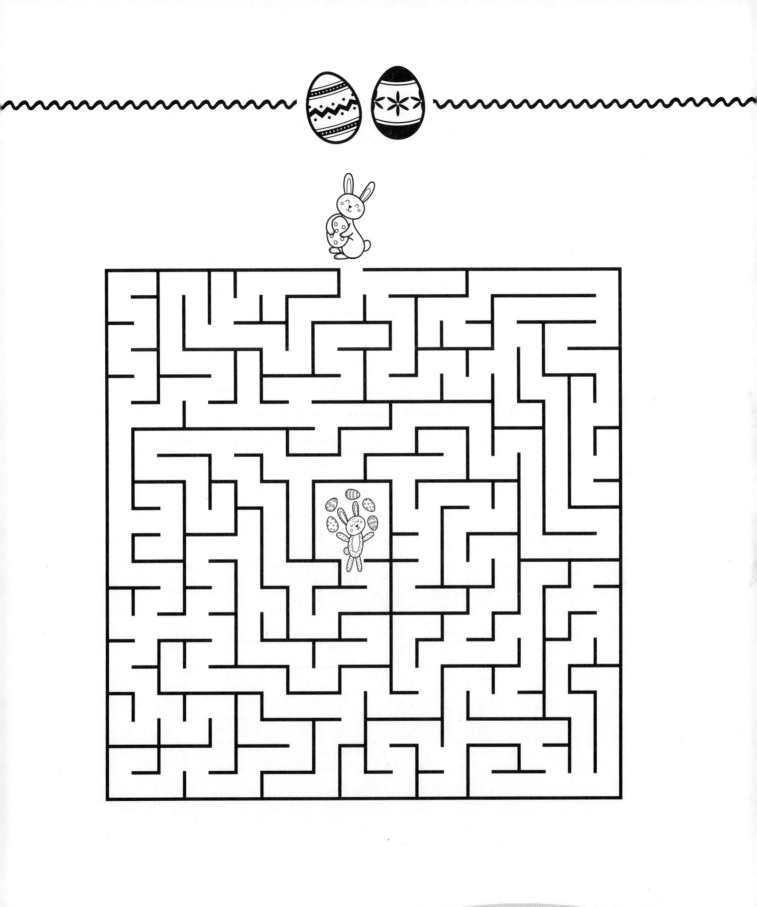

MAZE 119

MAZE 120

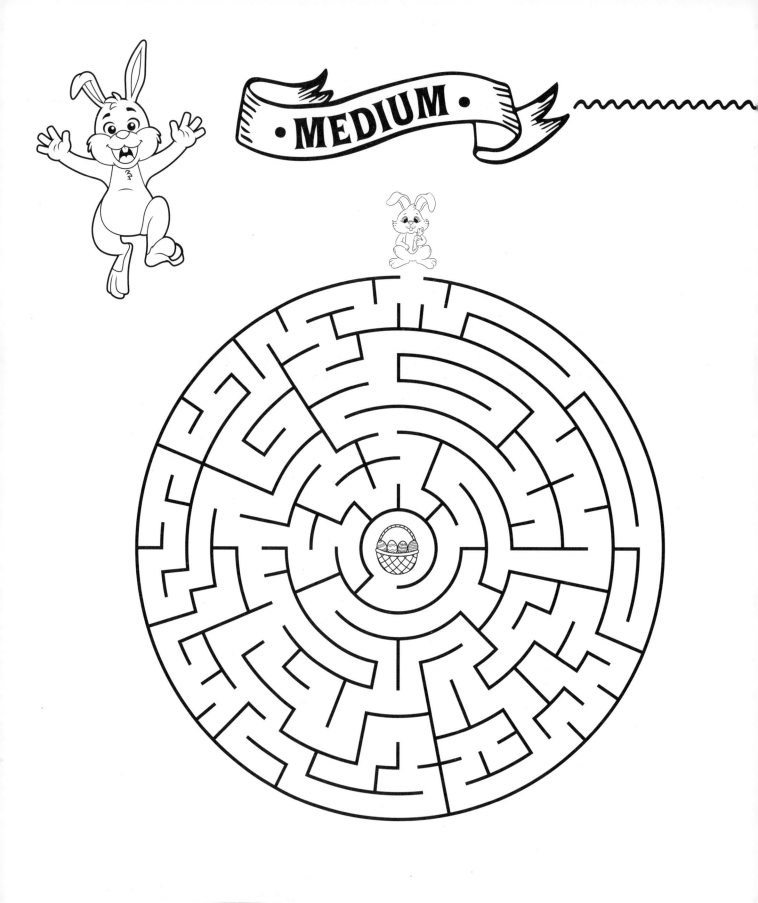

MAZE 121

MAZE 123

MAZE 124

MEDIUM

MAZE 125

MAZE 126

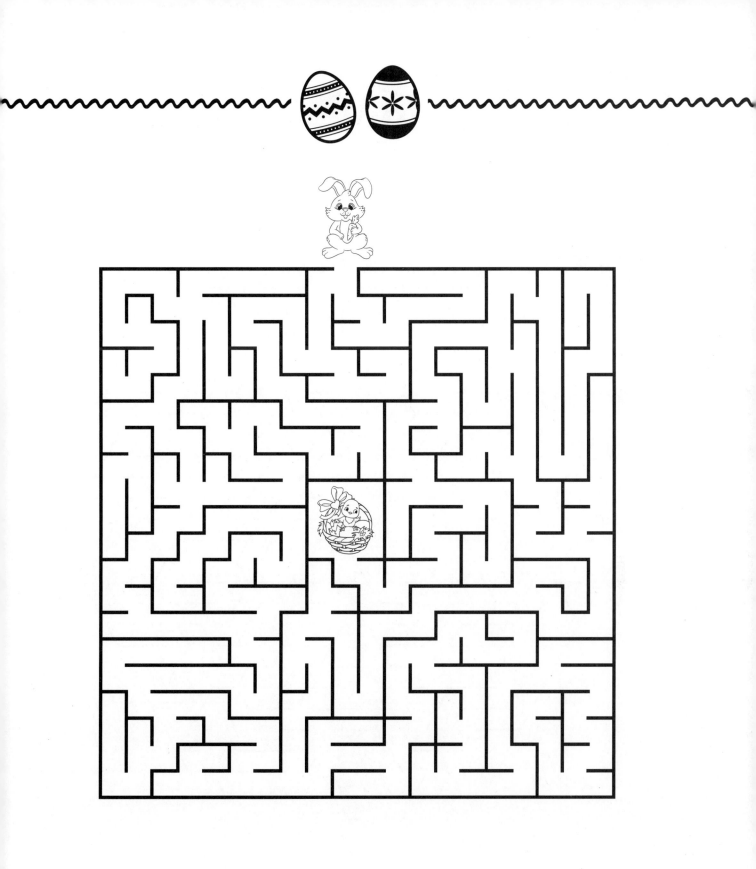

MAZE 128

MEDIUM

MAZE 129

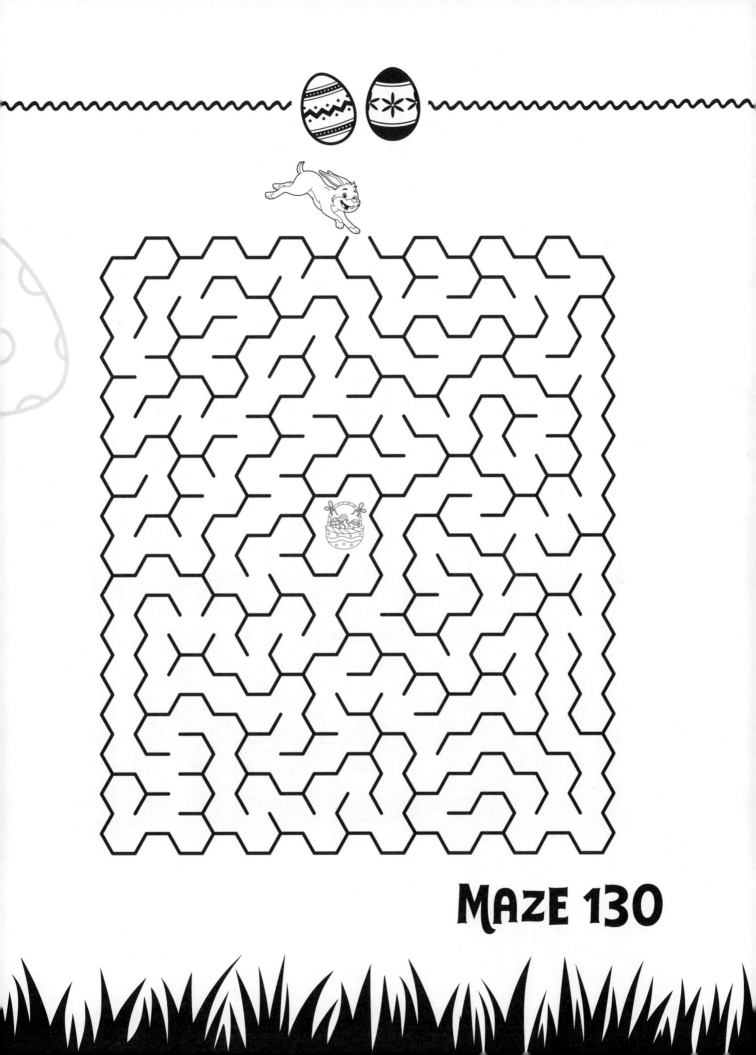

MAZE 130

MAZE 132

MEDIUM

MAZE 133

MAZE 134

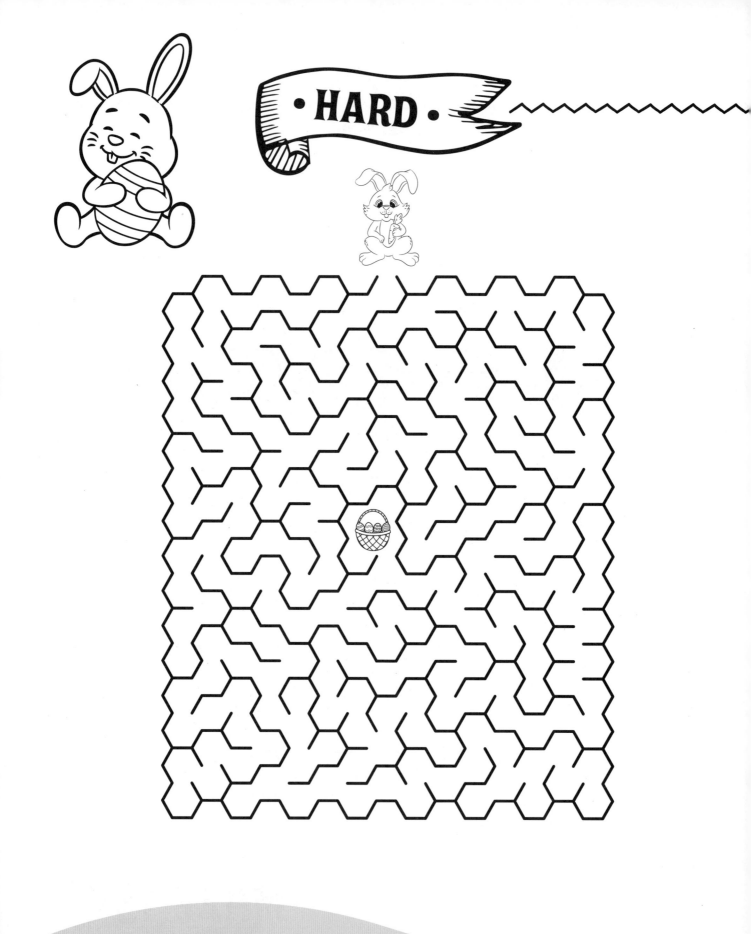

HARD

MAZE 135

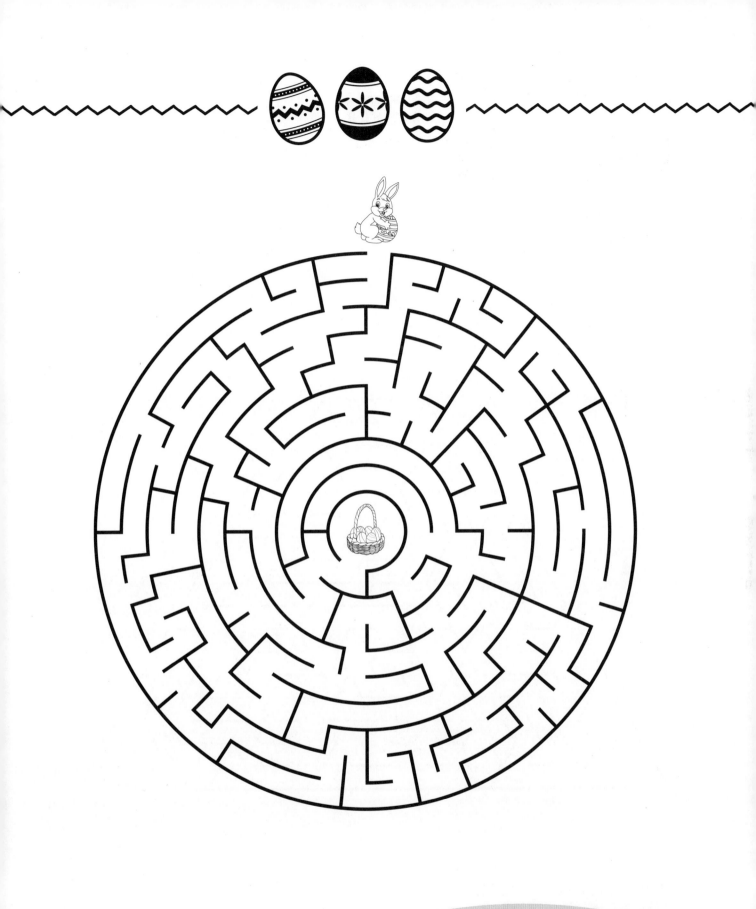

MAZE 137

MAZE 138

MAZE 139

MAZE 140

MAZE 141

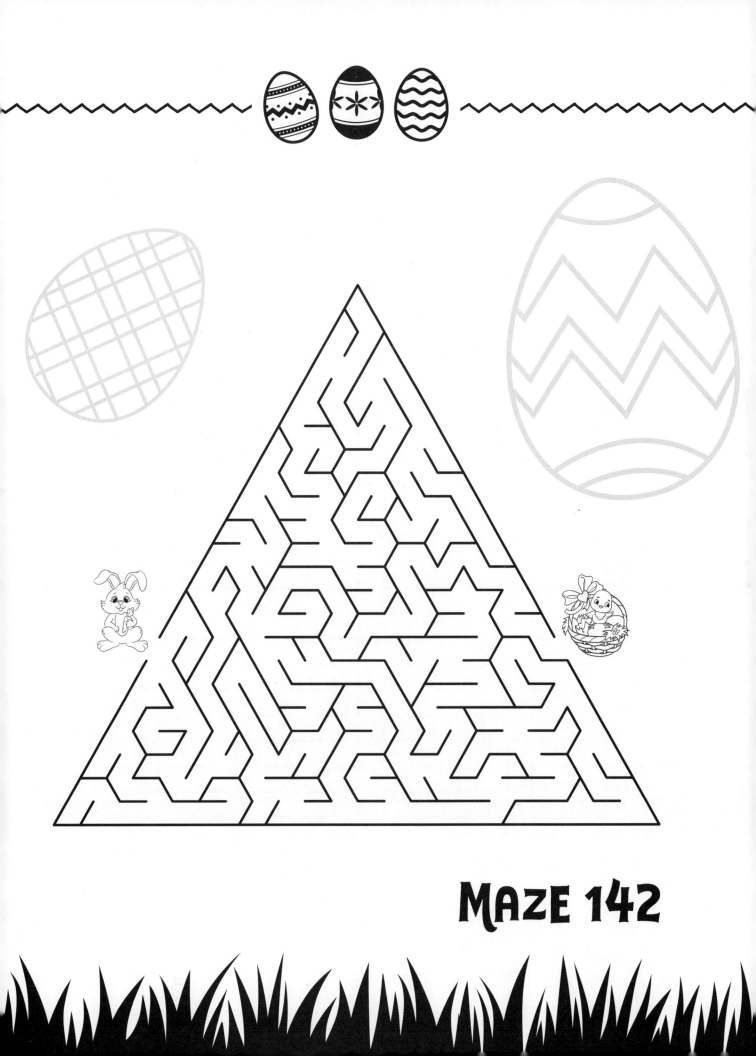

MAZE 142

MAZE 143

MAZE 144

HARD

MAZE 145

MAZE 146

MAZE 147

HARD

MAZE 149

MAZE 150

MAZE 151

MAZE 153

MAZE 154

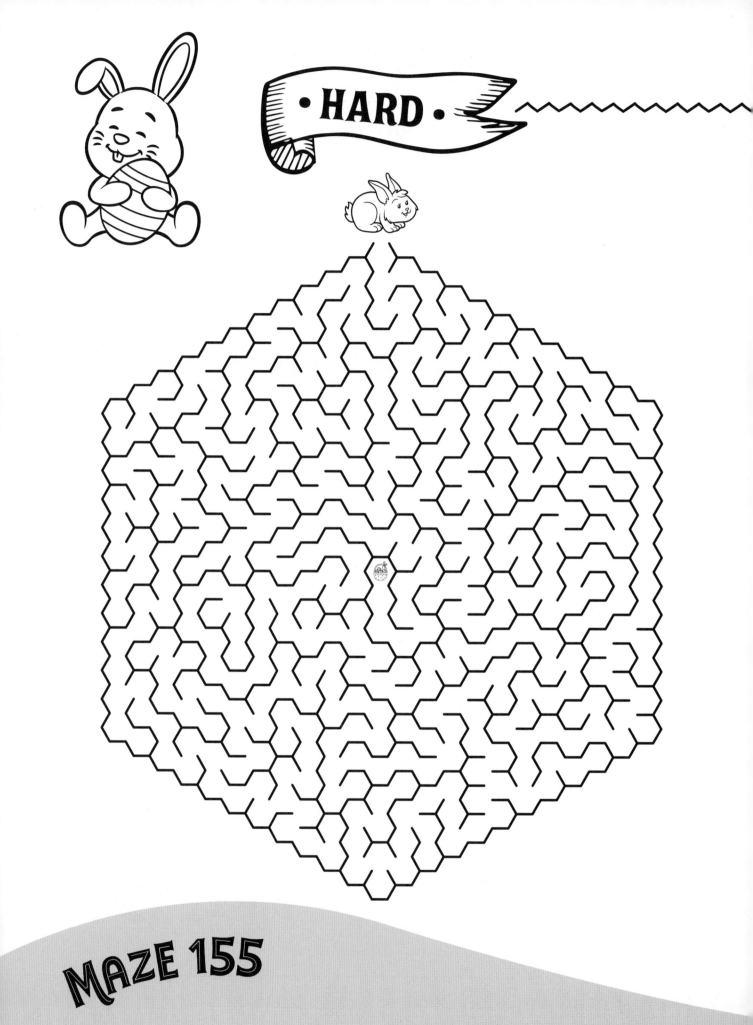

MAZE 155

MAZE 157

MAZE 158

HARD

MAZE 159

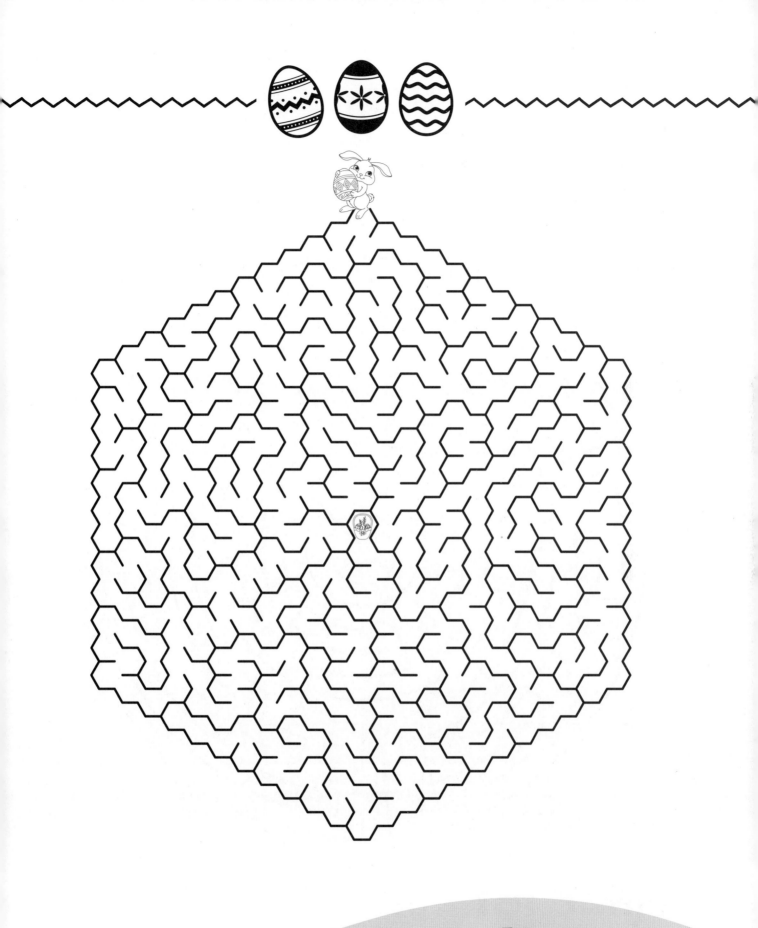

MAZE 160

MAZE 161

MAZE 162

HARD

MAZE 163

MAZE 164

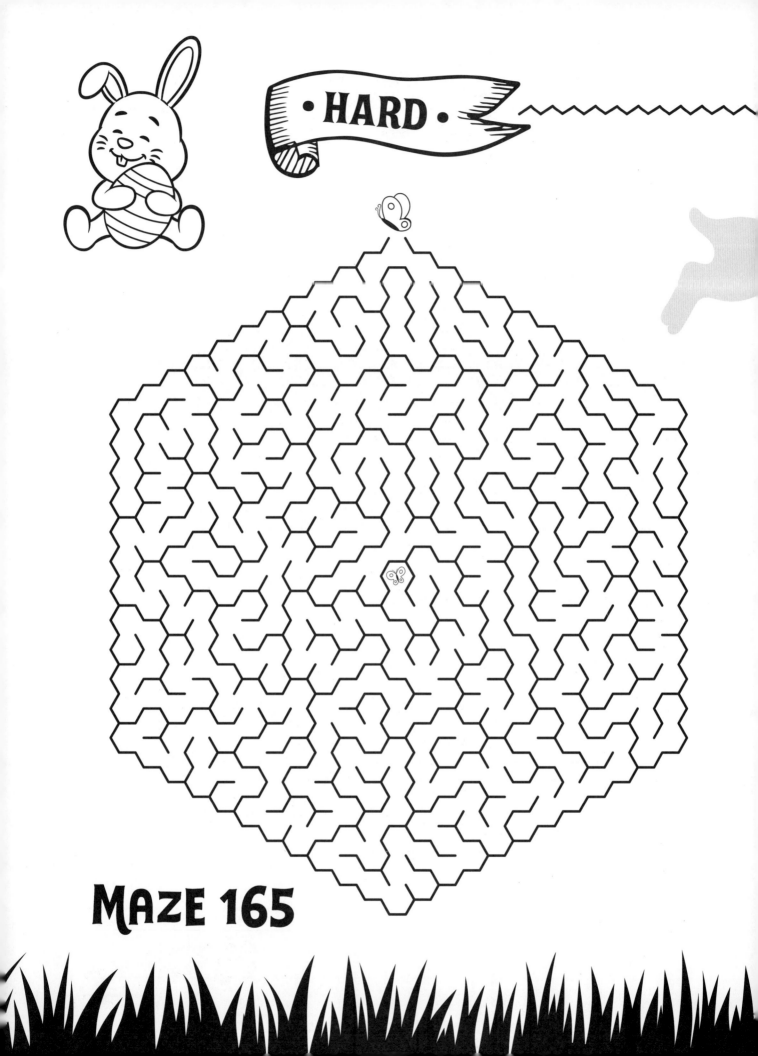

MAZE 165

MAZE 166

MAZE 167

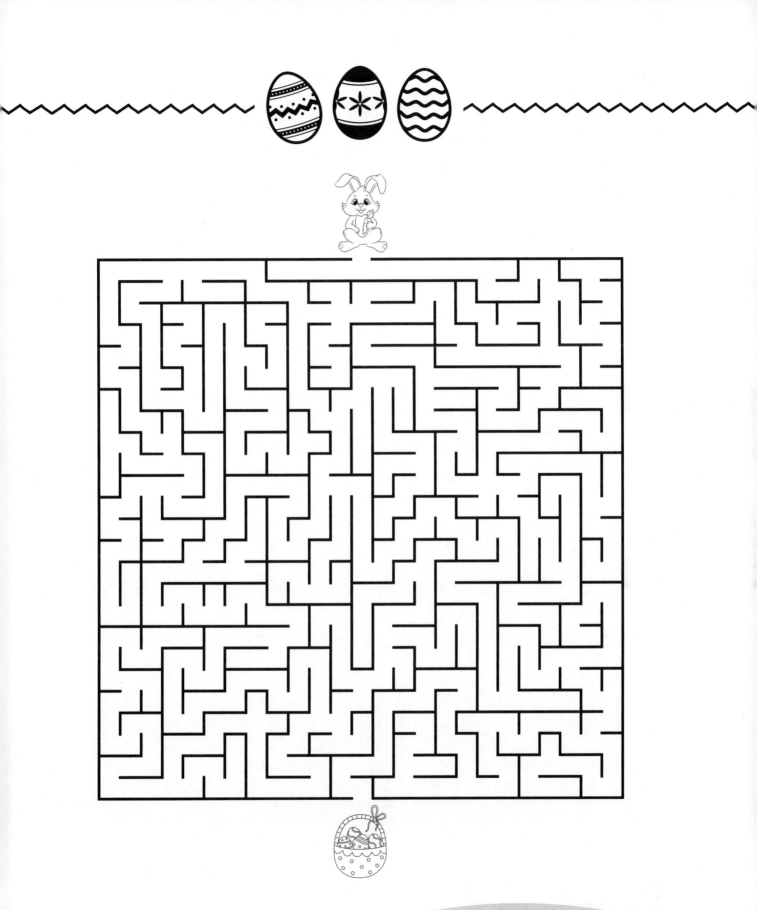

MAZE 168

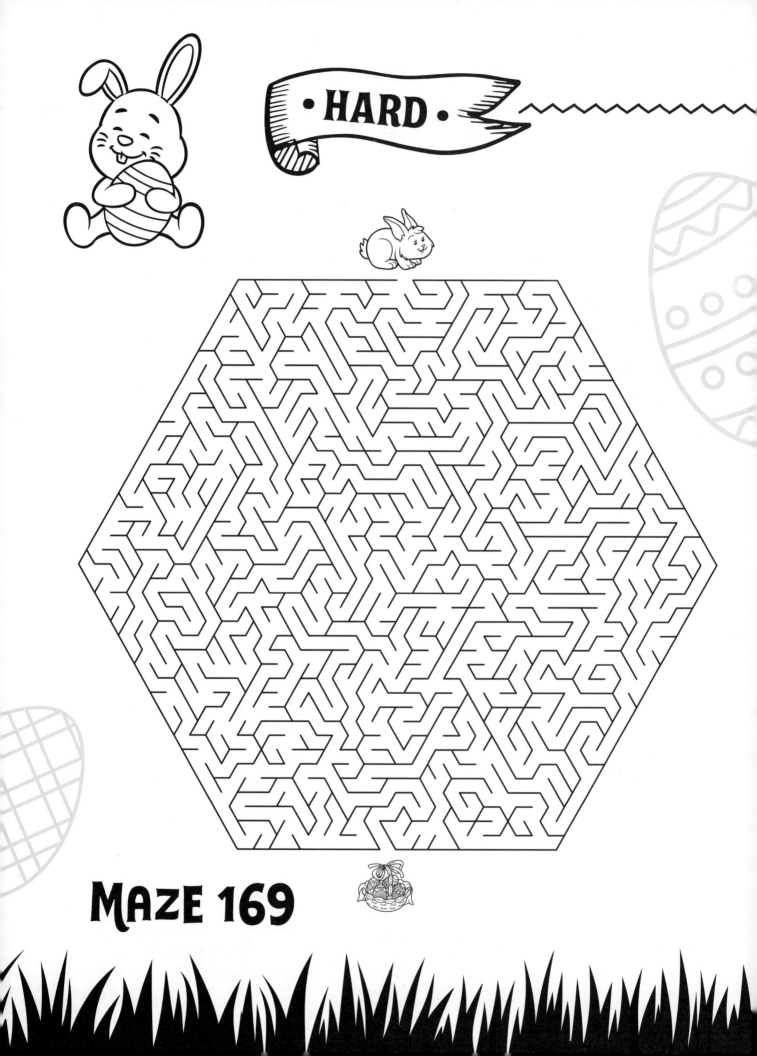

MAZE 169

MAZE 170

MAZE 171

HARD

MAZE 173

MAZE 174

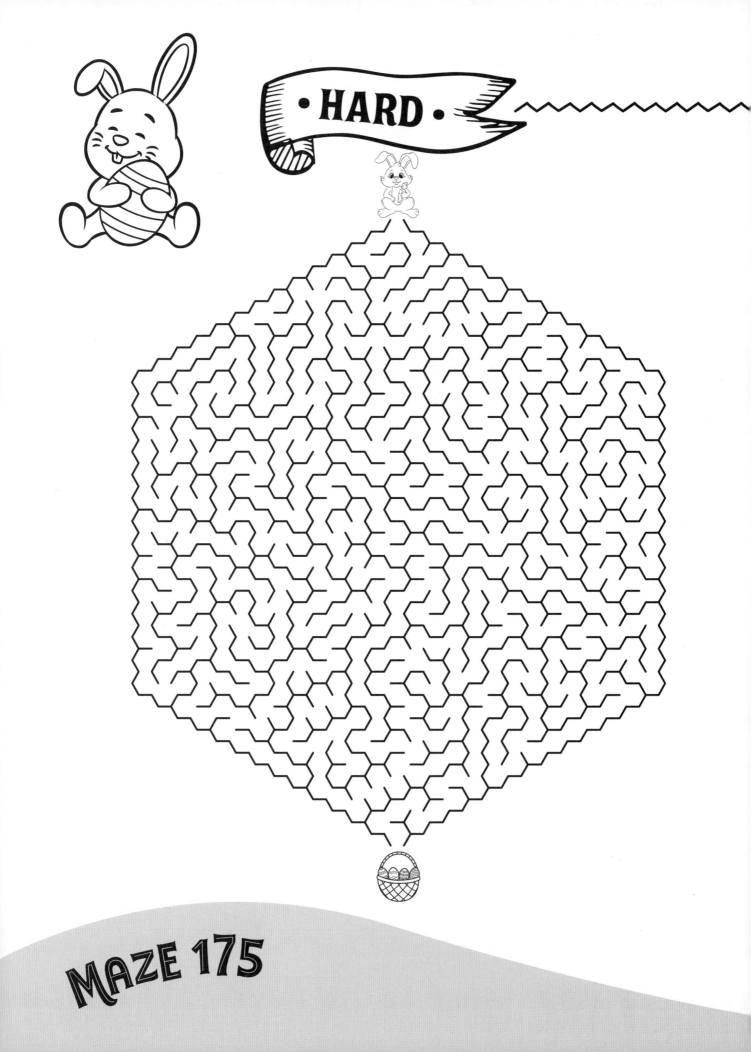

MAZE 175

MAZE 176

MAZE 177

MAZE 178

HARD

MAZE 179

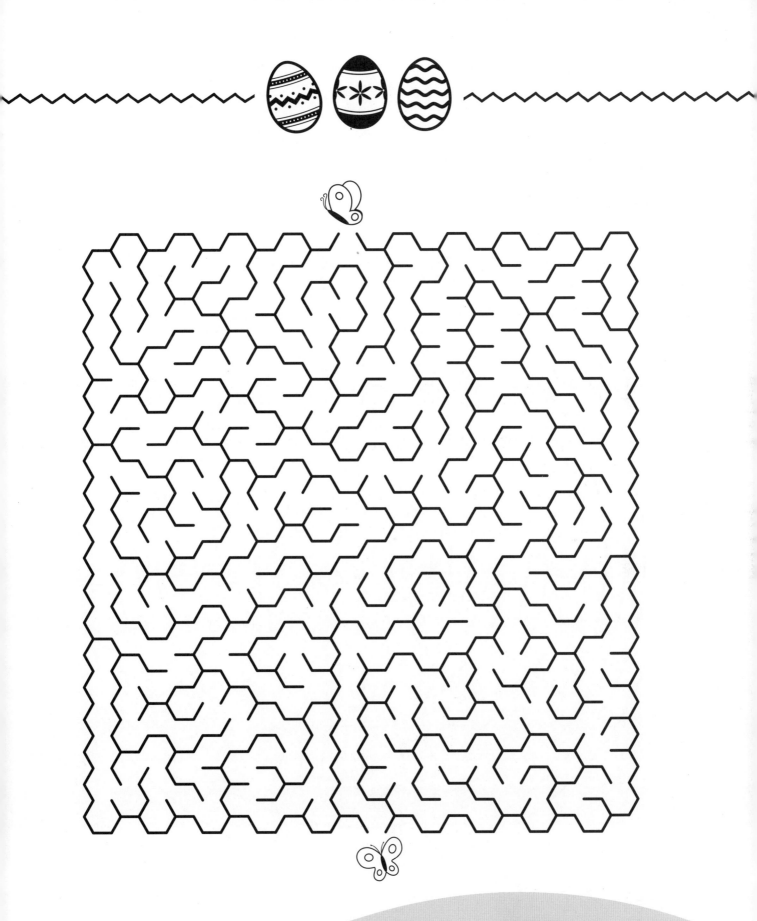

MAZE 180

MAZE 181

MAZE 182

MAZE 184

MAZE 185

MAZE 186

MAZE 188

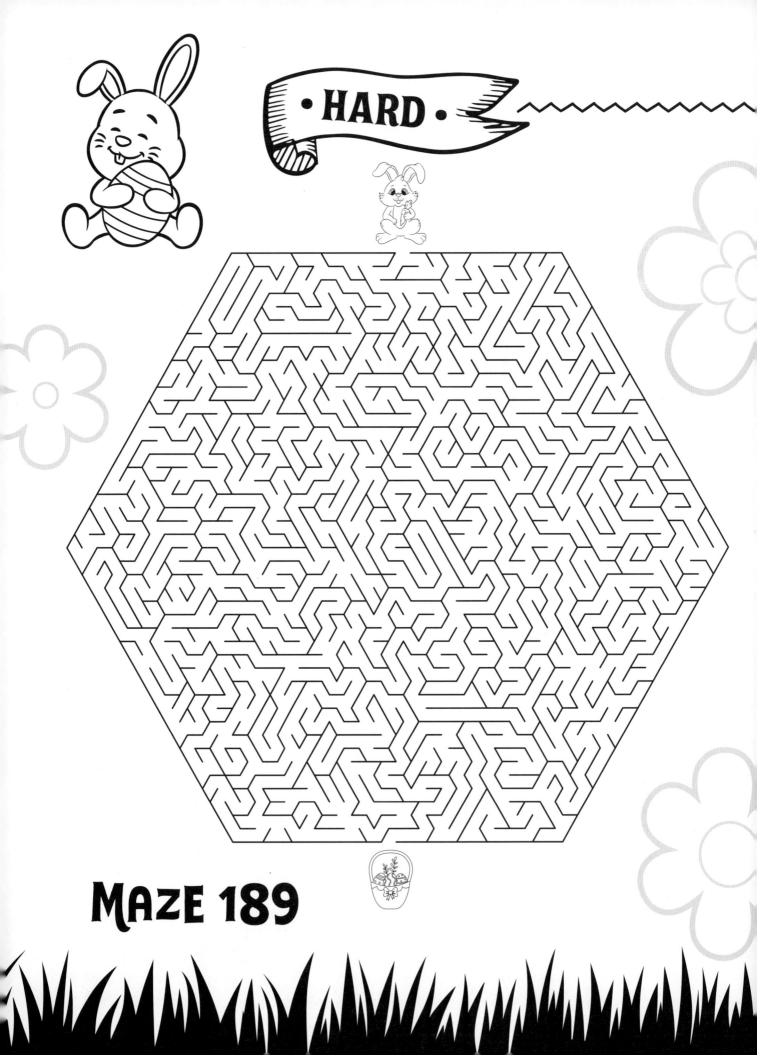

MAZE 189

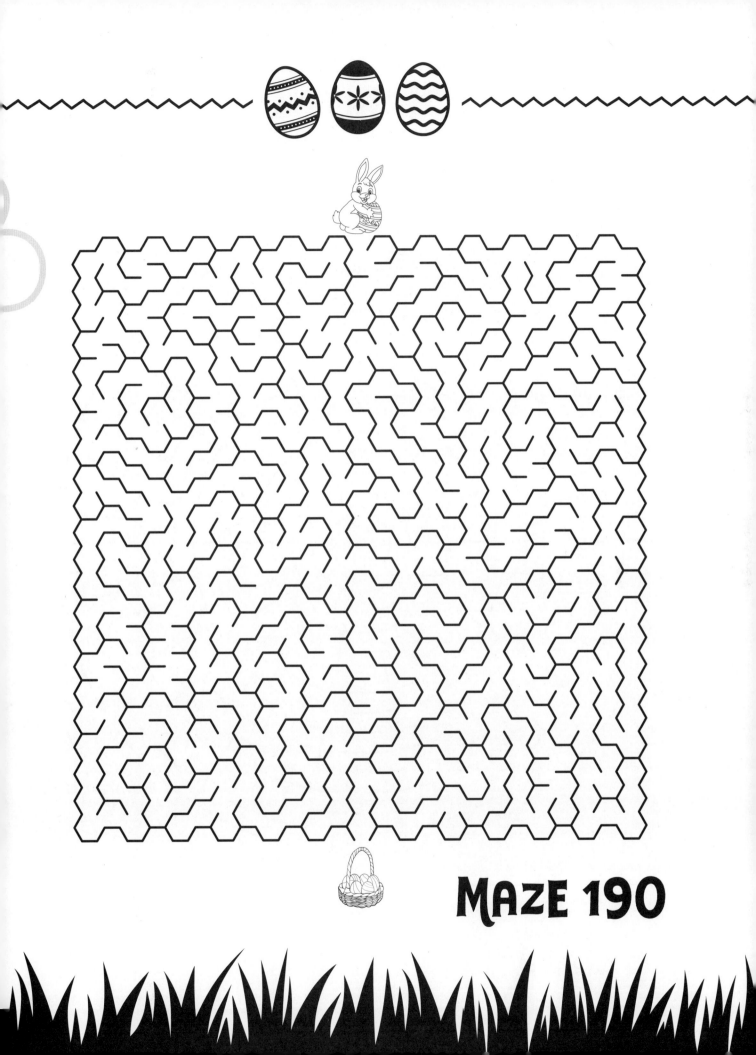

MAZE 190

MAZE 191

MAZE 192

HARD

MAZE 193

MAZE 194

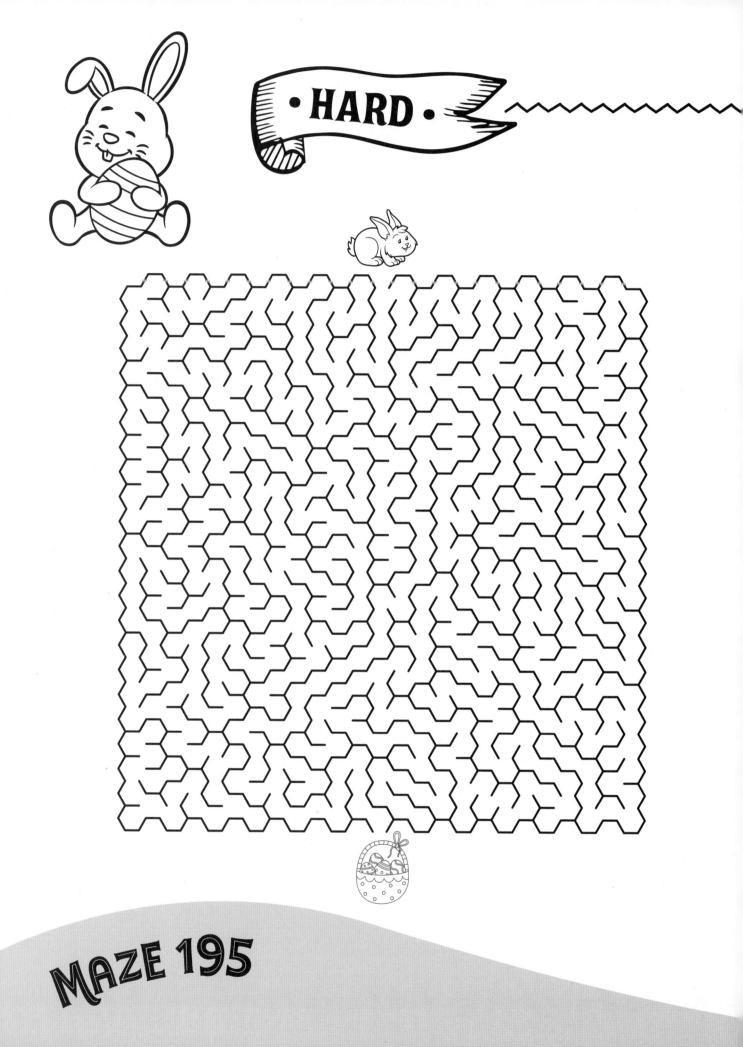

•HARD•

MAZE 195

MAZE 196

MAZE 197

MAZE 198

HARD

MAZE 199

MAZE 200

MAZE 1

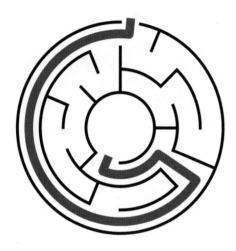

MAZE 2

MAZE 3

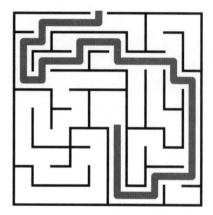

MAZE 4

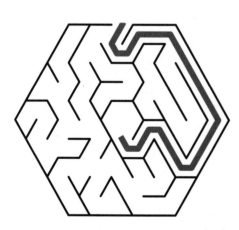

MAZE 5

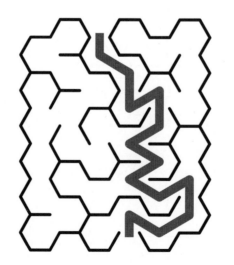

MAZE 6

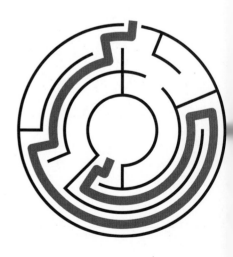

Maze 7

Maze 8

Maze 9

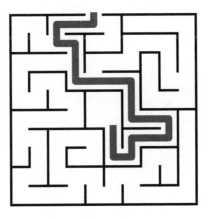

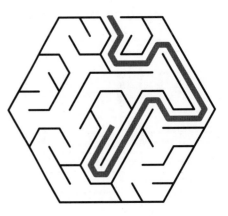

Maze 10

Maze 11

Maze 12

SOLUTIONS

MAZE 13

MAZE 14

MAZE 15

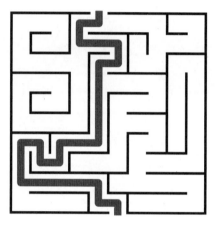

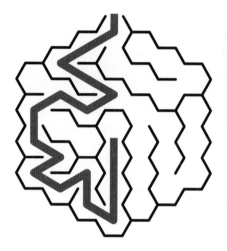

MAZE 16

MAZE 17

MAZE 18

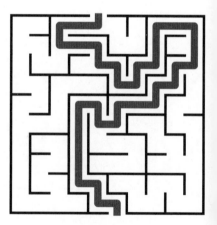

Maze 19

Maze 20

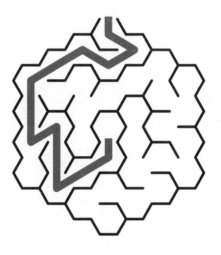

Maze 21

Maze 22

Maze 23

Maze 24

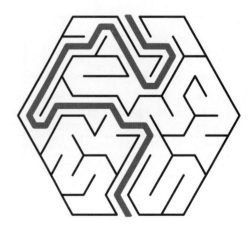

MAZE 25

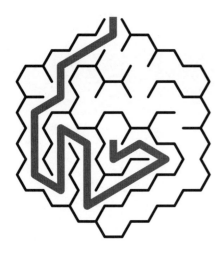

MAZE 26

MAZE 27

MAZE 28

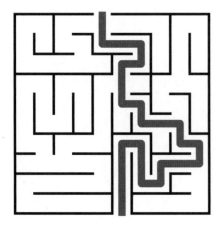

MAZE 29

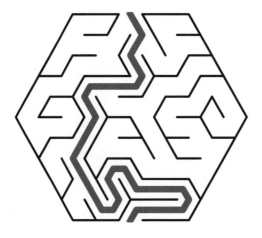

MAZE 30

MAZE 31

MAZE 32

MAZE 33

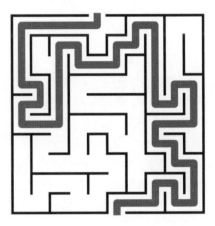

MAZE 34

MAZE 35

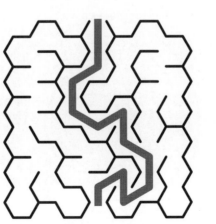

MAZE 36

· SOLUTIONS ·

MAZE 37

MAZE 38

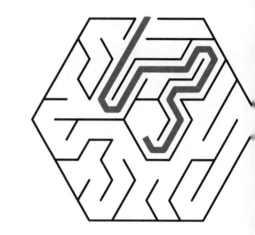

MAZE 39

MAZE 40

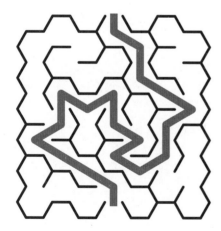

MAZE 41

MAZE 42

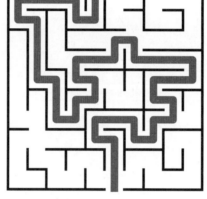

MAZE 43

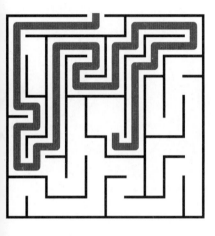

MAZE 44

MAZE 45

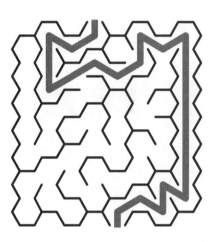

MAZE 46

MAZE 47

MAZE 48

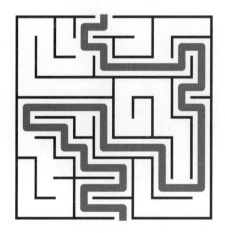

SOLUTIONS

MAZE 49

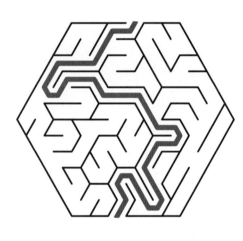

MAZE 50

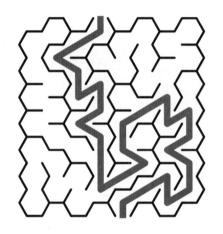

MAZE 51

MAZE 52

MAZE 53

MAZE 54

MAZE 55

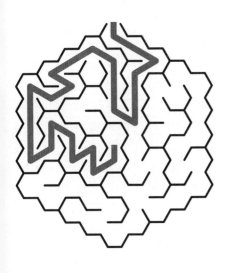

MAZE 56

MAZE 57

MAZE 58

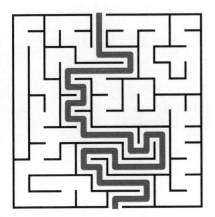

MAZE 59

MAZE 60

· SOLUTIONS ·

MAZE 61

MAZE 62

MAZE 63

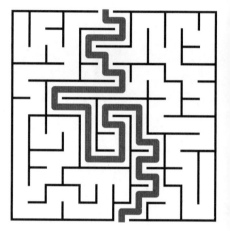

MAZE 64

MAZE 65

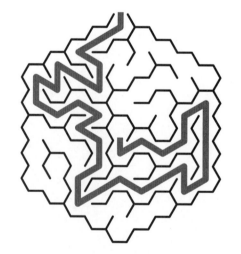

MAZE 66

MAZE 67

MAZE 68

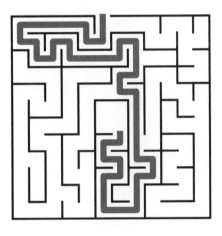

MAZE 69

MAZE 70

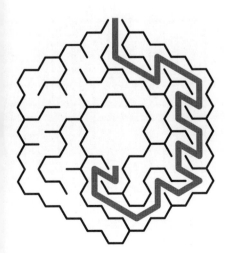

MAZE 71

MAZE 72

·SOLUTIONS·

Maze 73

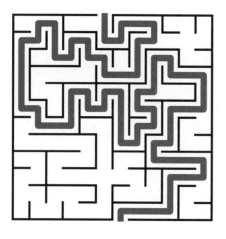

Maze 74

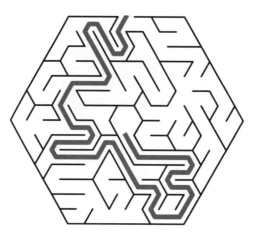

Maze 75

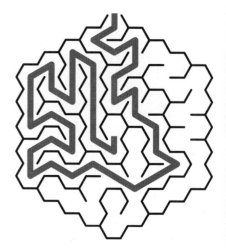

Maze 76

Maze 77

Maze 78

Maze 79

Maze 80

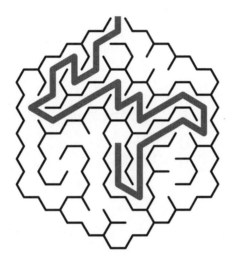

Maze 81

Maze 82

Maze 83

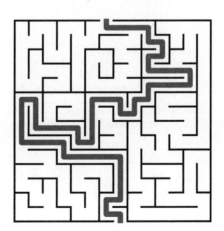

Maze 84

· SOLUTIONS ·

MAZE 85

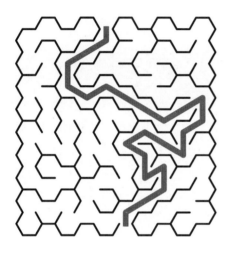

MAZE 86

MAZE 87

MAZE 88

MAZE 89

MAZE 90

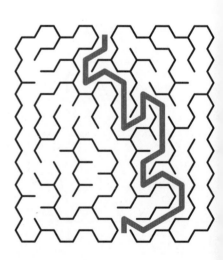

MAZE 91

MAZE 92

MAZE 93

MAZE 94

MAZE 95

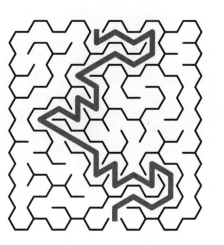

MAZE 96

· SOLUTIONS ·

MAZE 97

MAZE 98

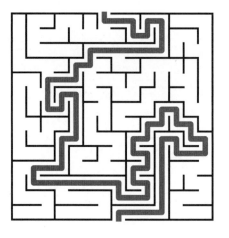

MAZE 99

MAZE 100

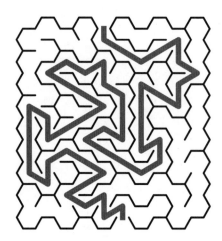

MAZE 101

MAZE 102

Maze 103

Maze 104

Maze 105

Maze 106

Maze 107

Maze 108

· SOLUTIONS ·

MAZE 109

MAZE 110

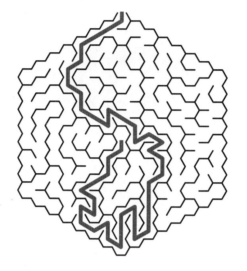

MAZE 111

MAZE 112

MAZE 113

MAZE 114

Maze 115

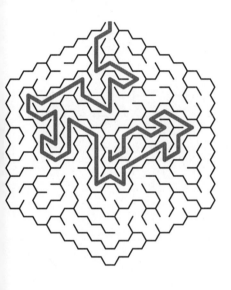

Maze 116

Maze 117

Maze 118

Maze 119

Maze 120

· SOLUTIONS ·

MAZE 121

MAZE 122

MAZE 123

MAZE 124

MAZE 125

MAZE 126

Maze 127

Maze 128

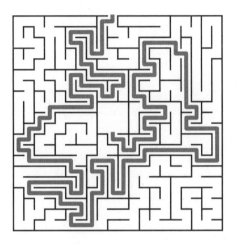

Maze 129

Maze 130

Maze 131

Maze 132

· SOLUTIONS ·

MAZE 133

MAZE 134

MAZE 135

MAZE 136

MAZE 137

MAZE 138

MAZE 139

MAZE 140

MAZE 141

MAZE 142

MAZE 143

MAZE 144

MAZE 145

MAZE 146

MAZE 147

MAZE 148

MAZE 149

MAZE 150

MAZE 151

MAZE 152

MAZE 153

MAZE 154

MAZE 155

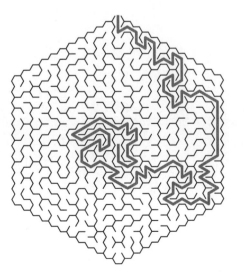

MAZE 156

· SOLUTIONS ·

MAZE 157

MAZE 158

MAZE 159

MAZE 160

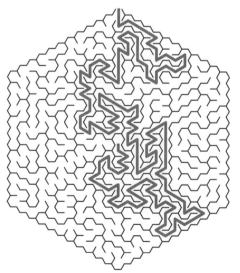

MAZE 161

MAZE 162

Maze 163

Maze 164

Maze 165

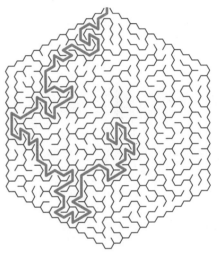

Maze 166

Maze 167

Maze 168

· SOLUTIONS ·

MAZE 169

MAZE 170

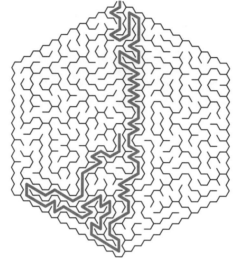

MAZE 171

MAZE 172

MAZE 173

MAZE 174

Maze 175

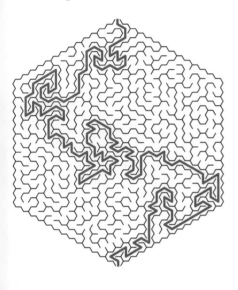

Maze 176

Maze 177

Maze 178

Maze 179

Maze 180

MAZE 181

MAZE 182

MAZE 183

MAZE 184

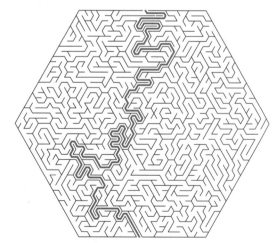

MAZE 185

MAZE 186

Maze 187

Maze 188

Maze 189

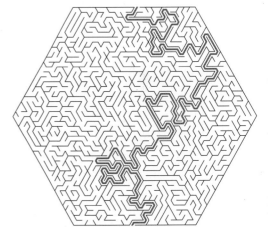

Maze 190

Maze 191

Maze 192

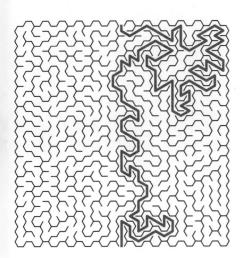

SOLUTIONS

MAZE 193

MAZE 194

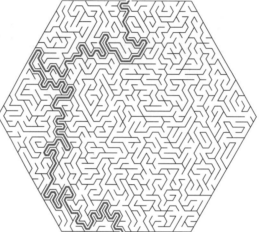

MAZE 195

MAZE 196

MAZE 197

MAZE 198

MAZE 199

MAZE 200

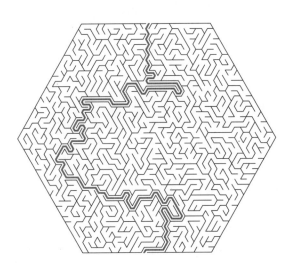

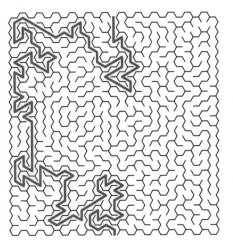

ALSO AVAILABLE FROM SKY PONY PRESS

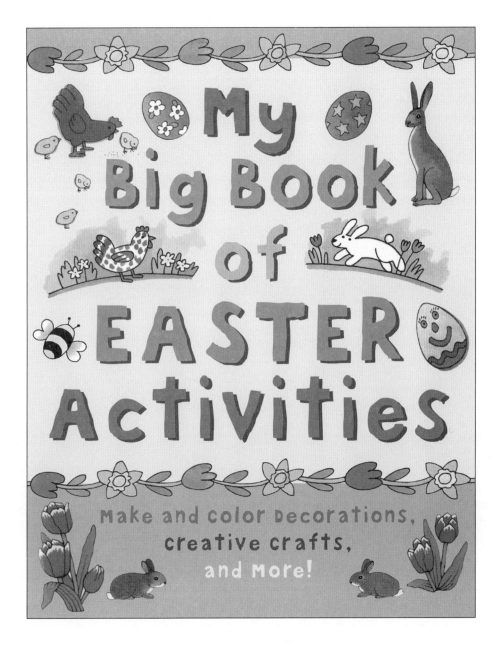